How Nonprofit Employees
can Unfriend Burnout

How Nonprofit Employees can Unfriend Burnout

Robert Lowery

HOW NONPROFIT EMPLOYEES
CAN UNFRIEND BURNOUT

iUniverse books may be ordered through booksellers or by contacting:

iUniverse
1663 Liberty Drive
Bloomington, IN 47403
www.iuniverse.com
844-349-9409

ISBN: 978-1-6632-4545-8 (sc)
ISBN: 978-1-6632-4546-5 (e)

Print information available on the last page.

iUniverse rev. date: 09/21/2022

CONTENTS

A NOTE FROM THE AUTHOR

Why This Ebook Exists

Hi there,

My name is Robert Lowery. I'm the author of this ebook and the CEO of RL Experience, which specializes in empowering entrepreneurs, small business owners, and nonprofits and faith-based leaders to grow personally and professionally. I'm also on the board of multiple nonprofits, but I used to work as an employee in the nonprofit sector. It was fun until burnout took over and made it impossible to enjoy the mission-driven work I was initially excited to do, which is why I wrote this ebook.

If you're passionate about working at nonprofits, I don't want that fire to disappear because you're too burned out to work. Instead, I want you to implement practices that will guarantee a sustainable work-life balance. And after many years of reflecting on how I could've done that and working directly with nonprofit employees to help them do that, I finally have the answers you need to make work fun again.

Ready to find out?

Let's dive into this ebook together.

Sincerely,
Robert Lowery

Chapter 1

Where Purpose and Burnout Meet

Why do you work at nonprofits?

If you're anything like me, it's because these organizations offer an opportunity to do meaningful work. Nonprofits seek to create positive change in communities, and this desire is what attracts job seekers to applications and employees to the office.

TIAA—a financial services company that specializes in medical, cultural, research, academic, and government fields—recently conducted a study indicating that the ability to make a difference is why eight in ten managers and three in four employees remain in the nonprofit sector. The same study also suggests that 74 percent of managers and 65 percent of employees have worked in nonprofit organizations for at least six years.

These managers and employees believe success comes down to the help they give. While compensation is important, making an impact is the primary reason these respondents entered the nonprofit world. And thankfully, their desire to enact positive change is being fulfilled.

According to the TIAA study, 97 percent of managers and 91 percent of employees think they're making a difference through their work. Seventy-three percent of millennial nonprofit managers even believe their organizations develop more opportunities for interesting and satisfying work.

Still, while the nonprofit sector is intriguing and offers the ability to do something meaningful, it's not easy to work in this market. Inspiring and implementing change currently requires many sacrifices that may sound tolerable in the beginning.

But what happens when those compromises start to add up and make work unbearable? From my experience, it leads to negative feelings and burnout.

Chapter 2

The Primary Source of A Nonprofit's Issues

There's one problem every nonprofit faces: consistently securing funding. It's from this problem that every other challenge gets its roots and nourishment to grow, and that's because funding is *that* significant of an issue.

According to a <u>2013 report</u>, the <u>Urban Institute</u> surveyed more than 4,000 nonprofits ranging in size, purpose, and U.S location. Based on the results, nonprofits—regardless of their particularities—struggled to secure funding to cover the costs of their services, and they frequently faced delays in payment.

Also working against nonprofits is their annual budgets, which typically don't exceed $1 million. Most nonprofit organizations depend on government funding, but policies constantly change, leading to shifts in funding priorities and rendering once-dependable financial sources non-existent.

Additionally, funders face immense pressure to reduce costs and tighten budgets, and the weight of this has led to the "nonprofit starvation cycle." It begins with funders' unrealistic expectations of how much it'll cost to run a nonprofit. Organizations respond by decreasing overhead and under-reporting business expenses. But this only re-creates the issue and allows funders to maintain the false expectations that started the cycle.

When the pandemic hit in 2020, <u>nonprofit</u> <u>funding challenges</u> became even more visible. Many of these organizations experienced significant reductions in total revenue and expected the issue to worsen with individual contributions and foundation funding.

Most of these decreases happened because the pandemic struck towards the beginning of the year when nonprofits were preparing to host their annual fundraising events. These gatherings are especially critical for smaller nonprofits that rely on these events as a major source of income.

For example, an organization that offers academic scholarships to Latina students in central Washington canceled its annual fundraising event because of the pandemic. The leadership team returned the money to funders, who usually spend $5,000 to $10,000. That's a significant amount of money from one event that could no longer happen.

However, canceling annual fundraising events wasn't the only reason nonprofits struggled during the pandemic. Unfortunately, in 2020, people viewed some nonprofits <u>as less essential than others</u>. For example, ones that focused on the arts or education weren't top of mind, while nonprofits that helped families eat and pay rent got more financial support from funders.

In 2020, health and human services nonprofit organizations experienced massive increases in their budgets. Philanthropic foundations and government institutions provided many emergency grants to these nonprofits, allowing people to receive quality assistance and support.

One organization attracted nearly $10 million in funding that went directly towards helping consumers.

Also worth noting is the increased funding Black, Indigenous, and people of color (BIPOC)-led and BIPOC-serving nonprofits received. Prioritizing these organizations and simplifying their application requirements for funding were top initiatives in 2020 for funders. These reduced restrictions empowered BIPOC-led and BIPOC-serving nonprofits to secure significant funding.

But despite these gains and funders' generosity, guess what? Nonprofits are already seeing funds roll in slower, and application and reporting requirements are becoming more stringent. Undoubtedly, things are returning to normal.

Chapter 3

How Insufficient Funding Affects Employees

The impact of little funding is like a domino effect. This primary problem affects employees in one way, then another, and then another, and the cycle continues.

If you work in a nonprofit, you know what I'm talking about—many of the issues I'm about to mention are interconnected and relatable. I've experienced them, and I've seen nonprofit employees deal with them time and time again. Even research validates that these issues are real. So if you've ever wondered if you're alone in what you're experiencing, let me be clear: you're not.

There are five problems many nonprofit workers face that stem from a lack of funding.

1. Low Pay Rates

If it's hard for nonprofits to make money, it'll be hard for you to make money. In the nonprofit world, compensation is low, so much so that research suggests <u>47 percent of employees</u> are unhappy with the pay ranges. Low salaries are especially hard to accept when employees at for-profit companies are making significantly more.

A recent study examined eight titles in the nonprofit sector. For seven of them, employees earned between four percent and eight percent less than workers at for-profit brands. The only outlier was marketing managers, who earned nearly 18 percent less than their counterparts.

Of course, it's easy to shrug this off by remembering the reason nonprofits are so great: they provide an opportunity to do meaningful work. However, it's hard to keep that top of mind when you can barely make ends meet.

Oftentimes, low pay rates can even decrease job satisfaction. When the BDO Institute for Nonprofit Excellence <u>surveyed around 200 nonprofits</u>, it discovered that 78 percent of employees believe pay is a "moderate or high challenge" impacting satisfaction.

2. Long Work Hours

What happens when people don't make a certain amount of money, even after mentioning their concerns to managers? They quit. This reality is true in the for-profit and nonprofit world. But when nonprofits are strapped for cash *and* low on employees, do you know who feels the brunt of that unfortunate circumstance? You.

In the nonprofit sector, it's normal to work long hours. Organizations in this industry are not quick to cut a program or decrease the number of people they serve to prevent employees from overworking. Most nonprofits face financial issues and the problems associated with having a small team by <u>squeezing more work out of their employees</u>.

Sometimes, you may work until nightfall, so inspired to complete the mission that nothing else matters. However, after months of doing this, long work hours can affect your mental, emotional, and physical well-being.

3. Multiple Responsibilities

When you're working those long hours, what kind of tasks do you handle? Are they the responsibilities you were hired to tackle? In most people's experience, the answer is no.

Handling <u>multiple responsibilities</u> is a common struggle for nonprofit employees. When turnover is high and there isn't enough funding to grow the team, nonprofits have to rely on who they have to get multiple jobs done. That means you may be writing social media copy one day and in the accounting department chasing down late payments the next. And when you constantly have to switch hats, managing your time well can become significantly tricky, elongating your work hours even more.

4. Lack of Training

When you're tasked with multiple responsibilities, the hope is that someone will train you in the areas that are new. But a lack of funding and a busy team doesn't make that easy or possible. Most nonprofits spend the money and time they have on providing services and quality care to the community they serve, which is very important.

Enacting positive change requires a strong focus on the people that need the most help, but sometimes, that comes at a cost. It can restrict access to training resources because there's not enough money to provide them or enough time to ask someone to sit down and train you.

The worst part is that this can actually work against a nonprofit's mission in most situations. Providing services and quality care hinges on having a knowledgeable, well-trained staff. But if employees are unsure how to handle certain responsibilities, they can't always provide a high level of support and excellence.

5. No Upward Mobility

One of the toughest things to accept about the nonprofit world is that there's little room for advancement, especially for workers who are people of color. A lack of funding means promotions are already pretty scarce—most nonprofits don't have the money to give someone the raise that comes with a new title.

However, when you're putting in long hours, juggling multiple responsibilities, and trying to perform with little to no guidance, there's always a slither of hope that you'll get promoted. But this opportunity is rarely presented to people of color.

A recent study examined the leadership teams at some of the largest nonprofits and foundations and found they were mostly homogenous. The findings indicate that 87 percent of all presidents and executive directors were white. Only six percent were African Americans, three percent were Asian Americans, and four percent were Hispanics.

These numbers can be discouraging, especially since George Floyd's death inspired many conversations about diversity, equity, and inclusion. The call for increased representation in leadership—and in every level of business—was louder than ever before. But a <u>new survey</u> found that "34% of employees, including 39% of leaders," believe that diversity, equity, and inclusion initiatives are a waste of organizational time, effort, and money.

Chapter 4

Too Many Challenges
Has Consequences

When the challenges you experience become overwhelming, two things tend to happen. One of them is negative feelings about your job. The position you once woke up eager to fulfill starts to feel burdensome, and talking about work with family and friends is no longer fun. Eventually, this disappointment is followed by the second consequence: burnout.

Herbert Freudenberger coined this term in the 1970s to describe an extreme stress condition that results in severe mental, physical and emotional exhaustion. Burnout is significantly worse than fatigue, as it makes it difficult to handle day-to-day tasks and cope with stress.

People who are experiencing burnout usually encounter a sense of dread when they wake up in the morning and often feel like they have nothing left to give. Sometimes, this leads to a pessimistic outlook not only about work but on life in general. A sense of hopelessness also lingers and makes it hard to become or stay motivated.

And if this sounds so extreme that a nonprofit worker could never experience it, think again. Some underline show that 30 percent of nonprofit employees are already burned out, and an additional 20 percent are close to burning out. That means 50 percent of the nonprofit workforce is on the verge of burning out or already at that point.

Maybe you're wondering if you're one of those people contributing to that number. Well, the good news is that <u>several signs</u> will indicate if you're burned out:

- **Isolation:** When you're experiencing burnout, you usually feel overwhelmed and stop socializing and speaking with loved ones and co-workers.

- **Escapism:** Dissatisfaction with your reality will make it easier to fantasize about taking a solo trip or running away. Sometimes, you may even turn to alcohol, drugs, and comfort food to numb the pain.

- **Exhaustion:** Burnout will make you feel emotionally and physically depleted. You may notice headaches, sleeping changes, stomachaches, and shifts in your appetite.

- **Irritability:** It's common to lose your temper when you're not your best. You may lash out at family, friends, or co-workers and find everyday stressors like unplanned mishaps when preparing for work and handling household chores annoying.
- **Illness:** Long-term stress conditions like burnout can weaken your immune system, making it easier to get sick. You might suffer from a cold or insomnia or face mental health conditions like anxiety and depression.

There are also phases of burnout, so it's important to consider whether you've experienced some of these stages. That way, you know where you might be headed if you're not already there. Keeping that in mind, here are the 12 phases of burnout:

- **Excessive Ambition:** If you're handling many tasks, you may try to tackle them by increasing your drive.

- **Pushing Yourself Too Hard:** Excessive ambition will demand you to work harder than usual, which could take a toll on your well-being.

- **Self-neglect:** As you start pushing your limits, you'll neglect self-care practices like eating well, exercising, and getting a good night's sleep.

- **Shifting Blame:** Instead of recognizing and admitting that you're pushing yourself too hard, you may blame others for your struggles.

- **Solely Focusing on Work:** When your job becomes your main priority, you won't have time for anything else like spending time with family and friends and enjoying hobbies.

- **Denial:** Your behavior will change as you become more burned out, but you'll likely blame others for your anger or impatience.

- **Withdrawal:** As your burnout increases, withdrawing from loved ones and rejecting social invitations will become easier.

- **Aggression:** Becoming increasingly aggressive with family and friends is a normal part of burnout and something you'll notice.

- **Depersonalization:** Eventually, you may start feeling like you have no control over your life and detach from it.

- **Anxiety and Emptiness:** In this late stage, you'll feel empty and anxious and may turn

to gambling, substance use, or overeating
to cope.

- **Depression:** As time goes on, life may not
  feel as important and lose its meaning.

- **Physical or Mental Collapse:** The inability
  to cope might lead to a more dire result like
  collapsing, requiring medical attention.

It's easy to look at this list and start panicking if
you're in the middle of one of these stages. In fact,
your initial reaction might be to follow your old
co-workers' lead and quit your job.

However, not all hope is lost. If you genuinely
want to continue working at a nonprofit, there are
steps you can take to reduce and prevent burnout
so that you enjoy your job again.

Chapter 5

How to Decrease and Overcome Burnout

While I no longer work at a nonprofit, I still work with people who do, and I tell them they must choose whether this industry is the right fit for them. Some people look at the issues, feel burned out, and quit their job. But others look for ways to reduce burnout, despite the challenges of working at nonprofits.

I support whatever decision people make, and I'll support yours, too. If you decide to leave the nonprofit world, I hope you find something you enjoy that's just as fulfilling but easier to balance. On the other hand, if you choose to stay in the nonprofit world but need tips on how to overcome burnout, you don't have to look far. Here are several strategies you can use.

1. Prioritize Exercise

Working out boosts not only your physical health but also your emotional health. And you don't have to exercise for an hour or more to feel these benefits. A short walk or a 30-minute workout can help you feel better.

2. Maintain Healthy Sleep Patterns

Sleep is the best way to help your body rest, and you shouldn't sacrifice it. With adequate sleep, you'll think better and have more energy to go about your day with ease. So, try to establish a relaxing nighttime routine to help you sleep better at night. Read a book, listen to soothing music, and put your phone away.

3. Have a Balanced Diet

A balanced diet is great for your emotional, mental, and physical health. One way to develop a great diet is to incorporate omega-3 fatty acids into your meals, as they're a great natural antidepressant. Examples of <u>foods rich in omega-3s</u> are fish, walnuts, and flaxseed oil.

4. Reach Out for Help

When you're stressed, don't withdraw from people. Having others that you can confide in and seek guidance from is crucial. A great support system will help care for you in difficult times, so ask a friend or family member if they'd be willing to do a self-care "check-in" with you every week.

5. Practice Mindfulness

Practicing mindfulness is a great way to help you slow down, stay calm, and focus. Mindfulness is all about concentrating on your breath and becoming acutely aware of what you're feeling and sensing without judging the moment. In the workplace, this can help you cope with stress and face situations with patience and openness without criticizing anything.

6. Be Honest with Your Supervisor

If you're experiencing burnout, speak with your direct supervisor. Let them know what's going on and why it's happening, and then try to develop a healthy way to move forward. Sometimes, transparency pushes managers to make positive changes for their employees.

7. Do Something Relaxing

After your workday, do a relaxing activity. It could be meditation, yoga, journaling, or tai chi. Regardless of what you choose, the goal is to find a healthy activity that will decrease your stress levels and help you unwind.

8. Reset Expectations

Overcoming burnout will require you to reset expectations with your employer, clients, and co-workers. And this shouldn't be a step that you're afraid to take. It's essential to decrease your exposure to job stressors if you want to prevent or eliminate burnout, so don't be afraid to have tough conversations regarding how much work you're willing to take on.

Chapter 6

It's Possible to Have a Long-Term Career

It's not impossible to have a long-term career in the nonprofit sector. If you want to continue doing mission-driven work, you can achieve that goal. But you have to make sure you don't compromise your health and wellness to make it happen.

Set boundaries, practice self-care, and be transparent with colleagues and loved ones when you start to feel burned out. These steps will increase your joy from working at nonprofits, empowering you to stay in the industry long-term. Even better, taking steps to overcome burnout has the power to help change the industry as a whole.

SELF REFLECTION QUESTIONS

Use the questions below to assess how you can overcome burnout while working at a nonprofit organization. Take time to thoughtfully develop your responses so that you have a solid game plan for how to take care of yourself.

1. What are three ways you can set boundaries at your job?

2. What are 3-5 things that you can do daily to enhance your self-care?

3. What specific foods will you start implementing into your diet to eat more balanced meals?

4. Who do you feel comfortable opening up to about your challenges at work? Write down

their names and set up a weekly check-in call with them.

5. What techniques will you implement to help you practice mindfulness?

6. What specific challenges do you want to discuss with your supervisor? Write them down and set up a time to speak with your manager.

7. What are 2-3 relaxing activities that you commit to doing regularly to help you unwind?

8. Whose expectations do you need to reset to help decrease job stressors?